The Social Media in Practice Excellence Awards 2019

An Anthology of Case Histories

Edited by Dan Remenyi

The Social Media in Practice Excellence Awards 2017: An Anthology of Case Histories

Copyright © 2019 The authors

First published June 2019

Disclaimer: While every effort has been made by the editor, authors and the publishers to ensure that all the material in this book is accurate and correct at the time of going to press, any error made by readers as a result of any of the material, formulae or other information in this book is the sole responsibility of the reader. Readers should be aware that the URLs quoted in the book may change or be damaged by malware between the time of publishing and accessing by readers.

Note to readers: Some papers have been written by authors who use the American form of spelling and some use the British. These two different approaches have been left unchanged.

ISBN: 978-1-912764-24-2

Printed by Lightning Source POD

Published by: Academic Conferences and Publishing International Limited, Reading, RG4 9SJ, United Kingdom, info@academic-conferences.org

Available from www.academic-bookshop.com

Table of Contents

Acknowledgements

We would like to thank the judges, who initially read the abstracts of the case histories submitted to the competition and discussed these to select those to be submitted as full case histories. They subsequently evaluated the entries and made further selections to produce the finalists who are represented in this book.

Judging Team

Val Hooper Associate Professor, is Currently Head of the School of Marketing and International Business at Victoria University of Wellington. Previously she was Head of the School of Information Management. Her cross-disciplinary background situates her ideally to study topics such as social media, which she has researched for many years.

Werner Krings Dr, has 28+ years of consulting, marketing and sales experience in cross-sector industries in Europe and North America. His background includes Fortune 500 companies. His research at Henley Business School focused on optimising B2B processes with Social Media Business Usage in a global software environment. Currently, he teaches at various international business schools.

Christos Karpasitis Dr, obtained his Multimedia & Digital Entertainment Bachelor of Science (BSc) in 2010 from Northumbria University, UK. He holds a Master of Science (MSc) in E-Business & Information Systems from Newcastle University, UK and a PhD in Web Media & Internet Marketing from the University of Central Lancashire, UK.

Introduction

Giving visibility to interesting or leading edge applications of social media is the objective of the Social Media in Practice Excellence Awards Competition. We have been looking for effective social media applications in business or in the public sector.

The call for case histories was announced in late 2018 and 18 submissions were received describing on an outline basis a social media initiative. 14 contributors were invited to forward a full case history. A panel of judges chose the case history finalists who are invited to present their work at the 6th European Conference on Social Media, in Brighton, UK in June 2019.

The emphasis of the successful case histories is on innovative, creative and effective social media applications and the finalists published in this book are demonstrating this. Submissions to the competition this year are widespread with contributions from Australia, Poland, Portugal, India and South Africa.

The initiatives are also diverse, and include a student communication project from Portugal, as well as e-assessments in Australia. Projects from South Africa, Poland and India also focus on the introduction and use of Social Media in High Education. And away from Education there is a case on the use of Whatsapp groups in staff development. Although the competition was open to social media applications from all fields it is interesting that this year it is dominated by educational issue.

Dan Remenyi
Editor

Social Media as a Strategy for Communication with Students and the Community

Manuel Au-Yong-Oliveira
GOVCOPP, Department of Economics, Management, Industrial Engineering and Tourism, University of Aveiro, Portuga
mao@ua.pt

1. Introduction and general description of the specific objectives of the Social Media initiative

"Social media is a subset of applications available on the Internet and the Web which directly facilitates communication between individuals and which generally results in knowledge sharing." (Remenyi and Greener, 2016, p.13)

The main objective of our department (DEGEIT – the Department of Economics, Management, Industrial Engineering and Tourism), the largest department at the University of Aveiro, in Portugal, is to continue to contribute to the standing of the University of Aveiro as being the best university in Portugal as concerns student satisfaction and student learning. Social Media, we have learned, is a tremendous vehicle through which to connect with students, as our case study seeks to show. Social networks make peer-to-peer communication easier – especially the exchange of messages and comments between members and users (Chaffey and Ellis-Chadwick, 2012).

This first semester of 2018-2019, in lecturing Strategy and Competitiveness, at the Master's level, I decided to use WhatsApp, Facebook, and our electronic newsletter and LinkedIn to communicate with students and the greater community. For example, we, teachers and students, sang a song to help charity. The designated organization to receive our help this year was AFECTU – which is a Non-Governmental Organization (NGO) which takes in and finds new owners for dogs and cats

1

which have been abandoned or have been victims of bad and aggressive treatment by human beings.

AFECTU has made a public request for help as castrating and vaccinating cats and dogs and generally providing for medical treatment is very expensive, especially for an organization fully made up by volunteers and with no official income. This charity effort was done as a way to emphasise corporate social responsibility (CSR) as a marketing strategy of organisations (in this case of DEGEIT), but also as a duty we have towards the betterment of our community. Our intermediate and final recordings were shared on WhatsApp, LinkedIn, and Facebook; and also in our university online newspaper - *Jornal UA Online*. Furthermore, we also used our Moodle e-learning platform to communicate. Students relate well to Facebook and to LinkedIn. I received many notes from students – in person, via e-mail and via WhatsApp, LinkedIn and Facebook – stating how much they enjoyed the semester and our different activities – including the welcoming of an invited speaker who gave two lectures on CSR.

Furthermore, using Messenger (on Facebook) to communicate is also a preferred avenue of communication by students. Indeed, e-mail is a channel used for very specific more formal communication, we found. LinkedIn and Facebook views of our CSR video combined are currently over 3,100 views (over 1.8 thousand views on Facebook and over 1.3 thousand views on LinkedIn, on February 25, 2019). Students also share more readily and pay more attention to social media than to other forms of communication such as the aforementioned e-mail and regular SMS texts.

Our final video was put together by a student organisation (Aveiro Smart Business) who did it *pro bono* for us, therefore with no charge. The spirits were very high after the recording go-live and especially as this was done during the Christmas holiday period and soon after that too (the video sharing occurred on Christmas Eve and during the New Year). WhatsApp was also good to keep in touch with the various singing elements of our group. Of note is that two students, who are semi-professional performers, were invited to help organise the singing sessions. One such girl in particular, Filipa, a singer in her spare time, gave the singing group cues as to when to start and when to stop singing the chosen song lyrics.

A link is provided below to one of our team building activities this semester - singing "Do they know it's Christmas?" By Live Aid. Link on Facebook (1,800+ views); link on LinkedIn 1,300+ views: https://www.facebook.com/ASolidariedadeEstaNoTeuADN/videos/361951 927921409/

An image of the Jornal UA Online piece on our singing effort for charity is included in image 1. This media article is potentially read by 15,000 students and 1,000 lecturers, as well as by other non-teaching staff at the University of Aveiro.

Image 1: An image of the Jornal UA Online media piece on our singing effort for charity

2. The infrastructure (i.e. people, systems, exercises, or perhaps hardware, software, if any)

After ensuring the necessary number of singer volunteers (who were also recruited from one of my classes), we had to decide upon how and where to record the practice sessions as well as the final "go-live" session. One lecturer decided to recruit a student organization – Aveiro Smart Business – which offered to help us pro bono. Thus, a good camera was used both for taking photos, as well as for the video recordings. My iPhone 7 was also available for recording alternate images – both photos and videos, including during the practice sessions. The material was all shared on WhatsApp, between the group of volunteers, and in the build-up to the final recording session.

The practice sessions took place in the music department, at the University of Aveiro, where we reserved a main recording room. The main recording session was actually done in the DEGEIT's amphitheatre (a room used as a classroom, but also for official receptions, and which has the benefit of having a large stage we could all stand on) – image 2.

Image 2: A photo of the singing group during the final take of recordings of the "Live Aid" song – in December 2018.

3. The challenges (how and when they were encountered, how they were overcome)

Online conversations lead to expressions of empathy (Rosen, 2012)

The communication of the initiative, to sing a song for charity, by students, lecturers and administrative personnel, revealed itself to be a challenge we did not expect to encounter. E-mails were sent to the department's list of students, lecturers and administrative personnel, by the department's central office. However, the response was very limited, as the e-mail sender was the Secretarial Office, and the e-mail seemed to go unnoticed by the majority of the "target market".

Unfortunately, as one student stated, "We tend to not read e-mails from that sender, as the content is mostly of not much interest to us". We quickly decided, given the low number of volunteers gathered, to advertise the initiative on Facebook. The results were very different and much better, and we could soon feel the buzz in the department around the upcoming event. There was much talk in the corridors of the department by people wanting to contribute with their efforts. "I cannot sing! But good luck!" was a statement repeated often, by more than a few well-wishers – mostly, in this case, lecturers. However, we had learned, the power of social media was undeniable, with e-mail coming in second or third as a preferred communication channel. A total of over one hundred volunteers, during the various practice sessions, and the final live recording, were involved, and the Head of Department, Professor Carlos Costa, was very pleased and proud of the final result (the video and the desire to help a NGO, in need, through added visibility and through bank transfers by donors) made available on social media.

4. How the initiative was received by the users or participants

When we feel empathy we are more likely to chat and spend time on Facebook (Collins, 2014, p.1)

Through social media we reached a greater audience. "E-mail itself which is not generally classified as a social media can be used to achieve the same sort of objective" (Remenyi and Greener, 2016, p.13). One student participant (Ana) sent me an e-mail simply stating: "The video turned out really nice. It was a great initiative. Merry Christmas!". A colleague, who participated, stated in an e-mail: "Congratulations to everyone, the result is very good! AFECTU does an excellent job, and any help for their cause is precious. I wish you all a Merry Christmas full of peace, health and harmony." In our WhatsApp "Christmas Song Live Aid" group it was more a matter of emojis being communicated – emojis being "any of various small images, symbols, or icons used in text fields in electronic communication (as in text messages, e-mail, and social media) to express the emotional attitude of the writer" (Merriam-Webster, 2019) – images being shared of thumbs-up, hands clapping, and smiling faces. There were also comments on WhatsApp such as: "Beautiful!"; "It is going to be a success!!!"; and "Our children [students] work wonders!". On LinkedIn someone who saw our video (a student named Ricardo) stated: "An excellent initiative! Congratulations".

We also requested that GRACE – a CSR association located in Lisbon, with close to 170 partner organisations – share our video on their online platform – which they agreed to do immediately.

The video on Facebook alone had 37 shares. The Head of DEGEIT commented on Facebook that "I am very proud of this and of a lot of other initiatives by the 'Ethics and Social Responsibility DEGEIT Commission', coordinated by Prof. Manuel Oliveira and with the active and creative participation of Profs. Maria João Carneiro, Miguel Oliveira, Joana Costa and Cláudia Silva. Thank-you to all of those fine voices at DEGEIT but not only to them… Merry Christmas!!".

Aveiro Smart Business, the student organisation that helped with the recordings and the editing of the final video stated: "Good morning Professor, we would like to again congratulate you for the initiative. We hope that your expected results are achieved. You may count on our help in a future project!"

According to the brand "Be Human – Solidarity is in your DNA!", a brand developed at DEGEIT, between students and lecturers, and on whose Facebook page the video was initially placed, the video and the publicizing of how AFECTU needs help was important so that more people would become aware of their hard time in implementing their mission to help badly treated and abandoned pet animals. The video was then shared by a number of individuals, including the Head of DEGEIT, as well as by the DEGEIT official Facebook page.

5. The learning outcomes – (what was achieved and how the outcomes were measured/evaluated)

"You are connected all day, every day, no matter where you go, unable to escape from the "plugged-in" aspect of today's culture." (Rosen, 2012, abstract)

The social media initiative described herein may also be seen as proactive online public relations (Chaffey and Ellis-Chadwick, 2012), which has several advantages: reach – when niche audiences are involved, or even when mass audiences are the objective – if the [DEGEIT] brand is

6

communicating a story of interest; and cost. In effect, the recording of the video had no direct cost involved, as all of the activity was managed by volunteers and implemented at (and by) the University of Aveiro.

The Jornal UA Online news item, the numerous messages exchanged on Moodle, with WhatsApp, on Facebook, on LinkedIn and via Messenger, were all done very quickly and for all to see. Social media are a phenomenon to be reckoned with, we learned, especially if there is a positive message being communicated.

The outcomes are essentially measured in views of the video (the reach) – and with over 3,100 views of our video, the production team was very happy. In future, we will seek to have sponsors of our charity activities so that besides greater knowledge by the public of certain problems, the institutions targeted may also have the benefit of solid financial support.

6. Plans to further develop the initiative

Corporate Social Responsibility efforts provide an excellent platform for additional interaction between lecturers and their students. Much of this interaction will occur outside the normal classroom environment, including on social media, which is seen to encourage additional empathy, so essential to the learning process (Bozkurt and Ozden, 2010; Collins, 2014; Kutlu and Coskun, 2014).

Thus, after this year's successful event, next year (i.e. before Christmas 2019) we intend to again sing a song for charity, to be shared on social media, while also launching a CD, with accompanying cover photos of the group of volunteers "in action".

The CD is to have a symbolic price of say 3 euros each, with the proceeds going to charity. At the same time, we hope to get sponsoring companies which agree to pay 1 euro for each visualization of the video on social media – Facebook and LinkedIn – to be given to charity or to support specific people in need. We thus intend very soon to engage GRACE – a powerful CSR group with important and powerful Portuguese member firms – to get the much-needed sponsors. A limit of perhaps 500 euros or 1,000 euros per firm would be established, so as to protect firms from a video which may go viral. Having teachers and students singing together for charity, on social media platforms, is not the norm for Portugal – and thus does generate some interest, as our latest effort showed. We have already secured volunteers to again sing for the upcoming edition of our "Christmas song 2019".

Acknowledgements

I would like to thank the Head of Department, Professor Carlos Costa, for all of his encouragement and enthusiasm for all of our initiatives which are related to corporate social responsibility; as well as for setting the example as regards social media usage. I would also like to thank the other members of the 'Ethics and Social Responsibility DEGEIT Commission', for their ideas and support - Maria João Carneiro, Miguel Oliveira, Joana Costa and Cláudia Silva – and for being open to social media in higher education. Finally, I would also like to leave a word of thanks to my colleagues Andreia Vitória and Mara Madaleno, for their input and dedication to our social responsibility efforts.

References

Bozkurt, T., Ozden, M.S. (2010). The relationship between empathetic classroom climate and students' success. WCPCG-2010, Procedia Social and Behavioral Sciences, Vol. 5, pp.231-234.

Chaffey, D., Ellis-Chadwick, F. (2012). Digital marketing – Strategy, implementation and practice. 5th edition. Harlow, England: Pearson.

Collins, F.M. (2014). The relationship between social media and empathy. Georgia Southern University. Master of Science Thesis.

Kutlu, A., Coskun, L. (2014). The Role of Empathy in the Learning Process and Its Fruitful Outcomes: A Comparative Study. Journal of Educational and Social Research, Vol. 4(2), April, pp.203-207.

Merriam-Webster (2019). Definition of emoji. Available at: https://www.merriam-webster.com/dictionary/emoji, accessed on 22-02-2019.

Remenyi, D., Greener, S. (2016). Social media and digital scholarship for academic research – A user's guide. Reading, UK: ACPIL.

Rosen, L.D. (2012). iDisorder: Understanding Our Obsession with Technology and Overcoming Its Hold on Us. New York: St. Martin's Press.

Author Biography

 **Manuel Au-Yong Oliveira** lectures at the University of Aveiro (Department of Economics, Management, Industrial Engineering and Tourism – DEGEIT), in Portugal, where he is an Assistant Professor. Manuel's interests are in strategy, innovation, social media, and corporate social responsibility. Manuel is the Director of the Master's Degree in Management and is also a member of the Executive Committee of his department – DEGEIT – at the University of Aveiro. Manuel has around 200 research publications.

Wiki and Blog e-Assessments: an Australian Perspective

Tomayess Issa
Curtin University, Perth, Australia
Tomayess.Issa@cbs.curtin.edu.au

Abstract: This study will examine the use of Wiki and Blog tools for e-assessments in postgraduate units at an Australian university. E-assessments are being introduced in the higher education sector as it has become increasingly apparent that students are lacking the personal and professional skills required for their studies and for future employment. Given the needs of businesses, students should acquire and enhance these skills for both their studies and the workforce since organizations worldwide require their employees to have certain skills. Wiki and Blog tools have become a vital part of teaching and learning, especially in higher education, as they develop students' skills, enable students to engage in independent learning, and give students access to new, innovative and advanced information as it becomes available nationally and internationally. Using Wiki and Blog tools in higher education can bring challenges to the lecturer and students 1) motivation, and 2) marking process, a rubric was used, which reflected the following criteria: content, organization (i.e. well-presented and organized), attractiveness/appeal, contribution to groupwork and discussions, and structure and quality of writing. The completion of Wiki and Blog's activities were an excellent and inspiring knowledge for the students and lecturer as students learned new concepts from their colleagues and benefited from the lecturer's feedback. The lecturer's feedback comprised formative assessment of the students' Wiki/Blog contributions, and this had two advantages 1): improving communications and collaboration between students and lecturer, and 2) enhancing students' subsequent Wiki and Blog submissions. In future, Wiki and Blog will be part of other units from different disciplines to strengthen the research goals and purposes.

1. Introduction to the specific objectives of the Social Media initiative

The purpose of using Wiki and Blog tools for e-assessments approach in higher education is to develop students' learning skills, promote strategies for independent learning, and facilitate access to new knowledge and information related to the various academic units. Furthermore, e-

11

assessment plays a major role in imparting and enhancing specific skills, both personal and professional. Currently, academics in the higher education sector are increasingly making use of technology tools such as Wikis and Blogs for the purpose of assessment. The main reason for utilizing these tools in higher education, especially for assessments, is that today's students are lacking several, necessary professional and personal skills. In response to calls from organizations and businesses, academics should take some responsibility for ensuring that students are adequately equipped with the skills required by future employers. Academics have begun to use technology tools such as Wikis and Blogs as part of their assessment approach to impart and improve students' skills for their studies as well for the workforce in future (Aral, 2013, Chuttur, 2009, Cole, 2009, Issa et al., 2012, Karrer, 2008, Mahruf et al., 2012).

These tools have been introduced in the higher education sector to advance and expand students' professional skills, namely: Reading and Writing, Research, Information and Technology, Critical Thinking, Decision Making, Digital oral presentation and Drawing (i.e. concept maps), and students' personal skills including: Motivation, Leadership, Negotiation, Communication, Problem Solving, Time Management and Reflection.

These tools facilitate and encourage greater interaction, participation, debate and conversation among students and lecturers when they are utilized for various assessment tasks, class events and activities (Issa, 2014, p. 13).

Additionally, several studies (Chu et al., 2017, Mi and Gould, 2014, Novakovich et al., 2017, Ruge and McCormack, 2017, Sancho-Thomas et al., 2009, Taraghi et al., 2009, Zein, 2014) have confirmed that the use of technology such as Wikis and Blogs will encourage students to become independent learners and will improve their academic and personal skills, particularly since it enables them to frequently access their teachers' feedback. The e-Assessments, Wiki and Blog are introduced in two postgraduate units namely: Green Information Technology and Sustainability (GITS) and Knowledge Management Intelligence Systems (KMIS). I started teaching GITS from 2011 until now, while KMIS from Semester 2 2018.

2. The infrastructure, (ie people, systems, exercises, or perhaps hardware, software if any)

Our Students are mainly from Australia, Asia (Including India), Middle East, America (North and South), Russia, Mauritius and other parts of Africa. A mixture of different nationalities and cultures is a significant characteristic of this lecturer's units, as all students are required to interact with and share their knowledge and skills, experience, and cultural perspective with their peers either during face-to-face interaction or via the technologies tools (i.e. Wiki/Blog- blackboard platform). This cultural mix assists students to learn from each other by sharing knowledge, skills and cultural perspectives and this leads to developing self-esteem, communication skills and self-confidence. To develop students learning skills, especially those of communication and interaction, students must complete a set of challenging activities via Wiki/Blog. These activities comprise: analyses and evaluations of real-life case studies nationally and internationally, the drawing of concept maps based on unit materials, and the sharing of cutting-edge information derived from current news items relevant to the unit material. Students are required to upload their work to Wiki/ Blog on the blackboard platform, as individuals or as teams to be evaluated by the lecturer based on the rubric; also, the activities are presented orally to the class, again by individuals or as groups. A mark out of 15% and 25% was allocated for students' contributions to the weekly Wiki/ Blog respectively.

Students' Wiki/ Blog contributions were checked by the lecturer twice a week, on Monday and Thursday afternoons. Students' submissions were graded according to quality not quantity.

Providing feedback via (by Rubric) Wiki/Blog is less time consuming, and improves communication and collaboration between students and lecturers, as both lecturers and students provide live feedback in relation to activities during the class, and this will improve and enhance teamwork and collaboration (Biasutti and EL-Deghaidy, 2015, Chu et al., 2017, Cowan and Jack, 2011, de Arriba, 2016, Ng, 2016). Integrating this assessment in postgraduate units will promote students' communication skills including writing, reading, debating, written presentation and oral skills and drawing (i.e. concept maps).

3. The challenges (how and when they were encountered, how they were overcome)

The challenges are marking e-Assessments (Wiki/Blog) and Motivation. To assess students' contributions to e-Assessments Wiki/Blog, a rubric was used comprising the following criteria: content (i.e. topic(s) is/are covered in detail with excellent examples and knowledge of subject matter is outstanding); organization (well-presented and organized, using headings or bulleted list for group-related material); attractiveness/visual appeal (enhance Wiki/Blog presentation, student uses excellent choice of font, colour, graphics, effects...etc.); contribution to group work and discussions (student contributes to and develops the class Wiki/ Blog, by providing her/his opinion regarding her/his peers' Wiki/Blog contributions); accuracy (student's observations and perspective were presented, explained and demonstrated well); structure and quality of writing (well structured (e.g. paragraphing, sentence structure, spacing, spelling, proofreading, no HTML errors in Wiki/Blog, i.e. broken links, missing images, above average standard of expression and presentation, excellent overall expression and presentation, accurate acknowledgement of sources). The Lecturer's feedback via the rubric encourages students to engage with the unit and will help students to provide an exciting, memorable and motivating experience. As for the motivation, the lecturer encouraged her students to participate and engage in e-Assessments, by completing specific activities by themselves or as a group. In the class, the lecturer plays a good role, as she checked and listened to every student contribution and discussion during the preparation stage and she provided prompt formative feedback to improve the student's contribution before the submission. After that, the lecturer asked every student to present their findings based on the activities and interesting research, to share their opinions and perspectives with their colleagues. This exercise encouraged and motivated students to complete their work with good quality and on time especially the shy students.

4. How the initiative was received by the users or participants

In our university, we collected two evaluation feedback to confirm if learning outcomes are met or not, both informal and formal feedback was collected during the semester to indicate students' perceptions of their university learning experience and included feedback about the unit and the lecturers' teaching methods.

Informal feedback is a teaching and learning innovation: during the semester, students are asked to provide anonymous feedback regarding the unit structure, layout, Wiki/Blog use, lecturer's teaching, assessments and how the learning experience could be improved. This feedback is intended to assist the lecturers to enhance/improve their teaching of the unit before the end of the semester.

The second method is formal feedback (eVALUate), which is collected at the end of the semester through the university's formal feedback process.

It is intended to gather and report students' feedback about their learning experience and gives them the opportunity to provide anonymous evaluations of the unit and teaching approach. Furthermore, through the reflective process, students offer their reflections and opinions on their learning, thereby improving their level of engagement with the unit.

Students remain anonymous and the reflections are collected during week four of the semester via the informal feedback. The formal (eVALUate) feedback is a combination of quantitative and qualitative responses; while the informal student's feedback is limited to qualitative responses.

Based on the formal and informal feedback students confirmed that completing e-assessments via Wiki and Blog promote their personal and professional skills. The students' informal feedback indicated that the use of Wiki in the GITS unit was very interesting, motivating, exciting, and drew their attention to several issues in local and global news items. Students provided the following comments regarding the Wiki exercise:

- Wiki as a learning tool is a good avenue for us to really practice intelligent and fast research, writing and thinking skills as they are given impromptu in class and you were only given minutes to create then present. The classroom presentation enables us to freely impart our views on the topics and in the process hone our communication skills. We really need to have proper communication as a team to be able to deliver. I guess in here collaboration, teamwork, and proper time management are indeed sharpened.

- Wiki assisted me to improve Professional skills: i.e. Improved my analytical skills with respect to being sensitive and being aware of the importance of a sustainable development and business strategies. It improved my evaluation skills while ensuring that I understood the basics of Green IT and Sustainability Helped me gain analytical technique.
- With the individual wiki exercises, I was able to improve expressing my ideas since most of the tasks required us to share our perspectives on different subject areas.
- The group activity helps to really get to know our classmates well, more than just classmates in class. Stronger bonds are built. For improvements, it would be good to have different groups in every activity for the group task to be able to connect also with others.

Regarding the Blog tool used in the KMIS postgraduate unit, students' informal feedback confirmed that this tool enabled them to have a remarkable and brilliant learning experience. According to both the students and the lecturers, the Blog tool assisted students to improve their personal and professional skills in communication, leadership, debating, time management, problem-solving and decision-making, all of which are essential for their current university studies, as well as the workforce in the future. The Blog tool in the KMIS unit has become very sophisticated; as students recognized and confirmed, it makes the classes more interactive, cooperative and fun. Students shared the following comments:

- The blogs are another crucial part of the [KMIS] unit; we can learn about the other's student's perspective, adapt more knowledge and improve the writing skills as well. These blogs help the students to share their knowledge, which makes our knowledge limitless because if we keep the knowledge limit to ourselves it will be limited only. Blogs are easy to access, and anybody can see the other's blogs work and grab more information.
- The debate was fun and forces you to argue the side of a topic that you might not necessarily agree with, while also improving our public speaking skills. I think it would also be interesting to see people's opinions in debates before specific content is taught versus after a lecture, to see how their mindset has changed based on what they have learnt thought out the class.
- Team work: During the in-class activities such as: group discussions and blogs, I must be a part of a team as there are some blog activities

that need to be done in a group. Here I learn my things such as how to collaborate different views in a team, leadership.

5.   The learning outcomes (What was achieved and how the outcomes were measured/evaluated)

The use of Wiki/Blog in the GITS and KMIS units encouraged students to let their voices be heard, and to give their viewpoints on various topics in groups or as individuals. All the activities were posted to Wiki and Blog and the lecturer provide her feedback using the Wiki/ Blog rubric. Students also shared their views via formal or informal feedback, about the use of Wiki and Blog in the GITS unit generally and specifically to learn the unit materials i.e. sustainability and Green IT. While, the KMIS students learned about various topics related to unit materials, such as KM tools and processes, and Artificial Intelligence (AI).

Table 1 shows the formal feedback (eVALUate) for the GITS and KMIS units. The data obtained from the formal feedback indicated that students were pleased and satisfied with the assessment strategies, including the e-assessments for Wiki and Blog, as quantitative results for the GITS and KMIS units range from 91% to 100%, which is considered outstanding in relation to the overall satisfaction and other aspects namely; learning outcomes (92% to 100%), assessment (91% to 100%), motivation (92% to 100%), and best learning (91% to 100%), are highest compared to the university average.

Consequently, the results from table 1 show that students were also very satisfied and pleased with the lecturer effective teaching and presentation style, as many of the students confirmed that her teaching is unique and outstanding in Curtin University, since the quantitative results for the best learning item range from 91% to 100%. Based on the formal and informal students' feedback, that their lecturer is very approachable and encourage students to complete their assessments on time and she provided formative feedback to assist students to understand the assessment requirements well and obtain the necessary skills from each assessment.

Table 1: GITS and KMIS formal feedback (eVALUate)

Year	Item 1 Learning Outcomes		Item 4 Assessment		Item 8 Motivation		Item 9 Best Learning		Item 11 Overall satisfaction	
	Unit	University Average	Unit	University Average	Unit	University Average	Unit	University Average	Unit	University Average
GITS unit										
2018	92	90	100	86	100	86	100	87	100	84
2017	100	89	91	85	100	85	91	86	91	83
2016	100	89	94	85	100	85	94	87	100	84
2015	100	89	100	85	92	86	100	86	100	83
2014 /S2	100	88	100	84	100	85	100	86	100	83
2014 /S1	100	89	100	85	100	86	100	87	100	84
2013	100	89	100	89	100	85	100	87	100	84
2012	100	89	100	85	100	86	100	87	100	84
2011	92	89	92	85	92	84	92	86	92	84
KMIS Unit										
2018	100	90	100	86	100	86	100	88	100	84

Students shared the following comments regarding the lecturer teaching style:

- Tomayess techniques in teaching is very effective. She interacts with students during lecture which is really good to maintain the class attention in learning. Running exercise in the middle of class is a useful method in delivering the learning objectives. She is very approachable and always reminds students about the upcoming assessments and helpful with queries regarding the assessment. She tends to be funny at times which is good to keep the class alive, since it's a night class which most of the students are hungry and sleepy. Keep up the good work Tomayess.

- She is brilliant teacher and very polite with all. She gives the useful feedback and keep updated us by sending so much emails. She always fixes meeting with student to discuss on their issues. Overall, she is excellent. Thanks

- Tomayess Issa is a wonderful teacher as she always encourages students to do the things in the right way and very supportive for students. she is a well organised teacher and communicate very clearly. We can ask anything for as many times we want. She is very cooperative. We mostly get immediate replies for our inquiries and she always happy to help before and after class if any student has any question.

- Tomayess is an asset to the subject Approachable Patient with answering questions Enthusiastic about topic, the passion is good for the topic Helpful in providing research direction and tools.
- Availability - Continue and Quick response for any query, any time. Her valuable and timely feedback helps a lot during study period, to complete the assignments on time, and with required changes. Feedback- Her feedback for assignments results or even during progress towards assignments are highly appreciable. She never said wrong to any argument present by students, although she corrects it. It helps to keep the student's confidence to take part in in-class activities and share their view. She is one of the teachers, to whom I will remember forever. Thank you so much Madam. Words end ohh noo.
- She is the best teacher I ever had. She always encourages and motivate more and more to the students to do their work perfectly. She never be rude or shout on the students for lots of queries. She response so quickly. I love the way she teaches. She is my mentor, guru everything.
- Her teaching method is very effective and clear because she always tries to give her best in the class. She always communicates with students to encourage them.
- Feedback is excellent as always. Always available to help when required. Engages the class in activities promoting collaboration.
- Tomayess is a good teacher she has good communication her teacher style is very good she is paying good attention on students. provide every reasonable knowledge to its student and understand the problems of the students.
- First of all, Tomayess is the only one through which we can expect feedback. I used to send her my work and start doing other work. No more than 45 minutes I get my feedback with so helpful guidelines. She was not the one who always want to get rid of e-mails. I love sitting in her class. I enjoyed a lot. I learnt a lot. I don't think so in this university no teacher is better than her. She is very helpful, supportive, kind, polite. Having great sense of humour. I don't know at what time she sleeps. If we e-mail, her mid night still she replied on time. Finally, U R NOT GETTING OLD:-)

- Most helpful TOMAYESS ISSA lecturer. NO words for her she is THE BEST. unit is interesting. A lot of new things, Sustainability issues as well as she changed my mindset through lectures of Tomayess. Participation in the class, the involvement of Lecturer and students creates learning environment. She encourages us to do something new and even every student try to do the same. She is the one who replied every single email doesn't matter how many emails we sent to her related to the assignment. News sharing, videos share related to the sustainability in the class amazing really opened the mind.
- It's been wonderful to have a teacher who is so passionate about the subject matter taught in the unit and so active and innovative in their methods of teaching. The care and support provided throughout the semester really showed me another aspect of learning that I will take with me into future classes and gave me confidence in areas of research and writing that I've not had so far in my postgraduate education.

In conclusion, based on the formal feedback (see Table1) and some of students' comments, the e-assessments via Wiki and Blog in GITS and KMIS allowed students to obtain the necessary cutting-edge knowledge and skills and develop their independent learning which these skills are needed for the current study and the workforce in the future. Finally, I provided evidence from my students, of my ability to develop, facilitate and run an informative yet enjoyable units that enhance student learning, engagement and their overall student experience; which has been sustained over time; and been recognised by the Curtin Guild. In 2018, I was the overall, university-wide winner of the Student Guild Outstanding Achievement in Teaching Excellence 2017 Award. Receiving this award give me more motivation, enthusiasm and inspiration to assist more students more and more. Finally, as an academic I have the responsibility to enrich my students' knowledge regarding my unit's contents, and to enhance and improve their professional and personal skills, by completing the assessments and activities. I achieved my goals, and the extracts supplied above are evidence based on formal, informal students' feedback and awards. I like my job, and I am happy to share my knowledge with my students.

Regarding the Overall Curtin Guild award, please check the following links:

- IT expert is Curtin's top teacher according to students
- Curtin's Top Teachers Chosen By Students
- Curtin University senior lecturer recognised by students with Outstanding Achievement in Teaching Excellence award

6. Plans to further develop the initiative

The study confirmed, sanctioned and endorsed that using e-assessment via Wiki/ Blog in postgraduate units at an Australian university enhance students' independent learning by motivating them to complete all class work and assessment tasks, improving their understanding of the course material, and giving them knowledge and understanding of cutting-edge developments locally and globally. In the future, the e-Assessment will be implemented from different disciplines in the university to strength the research outcome and adding real case studies to motivate postgraduate students.

References

Aral, S. 2013. Social Media and Business Transformation: A Framework for Research. Information Systems Research 24, 3 - 13.

Biasutti, M. & El-Deghaidy, H. 2015. Interdisciplinary project-based learning: an online wiki experience in teacher education. Technology, Pedagogy and Education, 24, 339-355.

Chu, S. K. W., Reynolds, R. B., Tavares, N. J., Notari, M. & Lee, C. W. Y. 2017. Twenty-First Century Skills Education in Switzerland: An Example of Project-Based Learning Using Wiki in Science Education. 21st Century Skills Development Through Inquiry-Based Learning. Singapore Springer.

Chuttur, M. Y. 2009. Overview of the Technology Acceptance Model: Origins, Developments and Future Directions Sprouts: Working Papers on Information Systems, 9, 1- 23.

Cole, M. 2009. Using Wiki Technology to Support Student Engagement: Lessons from the Trenches. Computers and Education, 52, 141 - 146.

Cowan, B. R. & Jack, M. A. 2011. Exploring the wiki user experience: The effects of training spaces on novice user usability and anxiety towards wiki editing. Interacting with Computers, 23, 117-128.

De Arriba, R. 2016. Participation and collaborative learning in large class sizes: wiki, can you help me? Innovations in Education and Teaching International, 1-10.

Issa, T. 2014. Learning, Communication and Interaction via Wiki: An Australian Perspective. In: KAUR, H. & TAO, X. (eds.) ICTs and the Millennium Development Goals. USA: Springer.

Issa, T., Issa, T. & Chang, V. 2012. Technology and higher education: an Australian study. The International Journal of Learning 18, 223 - 236.

Karrer, T. 2008. Ten predictions for e-learning 2008: e-learning technology [Online]. Elearningtech.blogspot.com. Available: http://elearningtech.blogspot.com/2008/01/ten-predictions-for-elearning-2008.html [Accessed].

Kebashnee Moodley

Mahruf, M., Shohel, C. & Kirkwood, A. 2012. Using Technology for enhancing teaching and learning in Bangladesh: Challenges and Consequences. Learning, Media and Technology, 37, 414 - 428

Mi, M. & Gould, D. 2014. Wiki Technology Enhanced Group Project to Promote Active Learning in a Neuroscience Course for First-Year Medical Students: An Exploratory Study. Medical Reference Services Quarterly, 33, 125-135.

Ng, E. M. 2016. Fostering pre-service teachers' self-regulated learning through self-and peer assessment of wiki projects. Computers & Education, 98, 180-191.

Novakovich, J., Miah, S. & Shaw, S. 2017. Designing curriculum to shape professional social media skills and identity in virtual communities of practice. Computers & Education, 104, 65-90.

Ruge, G. & Mccormack, C. 2017. Building and construction students' skills development for employability—reframing assessment for learning in discipline-specific contexts. Architectural Engineering and Design Management, 13, 1-19.

Sancho-Thomas, P., Fuentes-Fernandez, R. & Fernandez-Manjon, B. 2009. Learning Teamwork Skills in University Programming Courses. Computers and Education 53, 517 - 531

Taraghi, B., Ebner, M. & Schaffert, S. Personal learning environments for higher education: A mashup based widget concept. F. Wild, M. Kalz, M. Palmér, & D. Müler (Éd.), Mash-Up Personal Learning Environments: Proceedings of the Workshop in conjunction with the 4th European Conference on Technology-Enhanced Learning (ECTEL'09), 2009. Citeseer, 15-22.

Zein, R. 2014. Explorative Study on the Ways of using Blogs and Wikis as Teaching and Learning Tools in Mathematics. In: SEARSON, M. & OCHOA, M. N. (eds.) Society for Information Technology & Teacher Education International Conference 2014. Jacksonville, Florida, United States: AACE.

Author Biography

Dr. Tomayess Issa is a Senior Lecturer in Curtin University/Australia, completed her PhD in Web Development and Human Factors. Demonstrated strong abilities to supervise PhD, MPhil and Masters' dissertations. Recipient of several awards for excellence in Teaching, including the Curtin Guild Award and the Students' Guild Outstanding Achievement in Teaching Excellence Award.

Perceived Usefulness Factors Influencing the Usage of Web 2.0 Tools in Higher Education

Kebashnee Moodley
Pearson Institute of Higher Education, South Africa
kebashnee.moodley@pearson.com

Abstract: The purpose of this study was to investigate the perceived usefulness factors that influence the usage of Web 2.0 tools among academics in higher education in South Africa. Web 2.0 technology tools have potential for teaching and learning, but currently there is a low rate of usage in higher education in South Africa (Yadav & Patwardhan, 2016). Therefore, this study examined the current situation of Web 2.0 technology tools at private, South African higher education institution (Pearson Institute of Higher Education) in Gauteng. The main research objective was to determine the perceived usefulness factors that influence the usage of Web 2.0 tools in higher education. The current level of usage of Web 2.0 technology tools are low at Pearson Institute of Higher Education. A total of 7% of academics at Pearson Institute of Higher Education make use of Web 2.0 tools in education. Individual factors (barriers) was one of the main factors that influenced the usage of Web 2.0 tools in higher education; organisational factors (training and support) is crucial for the successful usage of Web 2.0 tools; academics agree on the different perceived usefulness that exist to enhance and supplement traditional learning; perceived quality characteristic factors (ease of use) also contributed towards the usage of using Web 2.0 tools in teaching and learning. This study contributed to the general area of technology integration in education. It provided insight into the perceived usefulness factors predicting usage of Web 2.0 tools in higher education to supplement traditional teaching approach.

Keywords: Web 2.0 tools, Web 2.0 usage, higher education, academics, perceived usefulness, pedagogical characteristics of Web 2.0 tools.

1. Introduction to the specific objectives of the Social Media initiative

The advancement of technology has grown at such a rapid rate and has become such a common place for students that it would be ideal for academics to adopt technology in higher education (Bubaš, Ćorić and Orehovački, 2011).

Technology can be an enabler for academic staff to develop and broaden their teaching skills but this requires that the curriculum be redesigned to accommodate for these tools. The aim of this initiative was to uncover the factors influencing the integration of learning technologies in the classroom. It sought to measure the degree of technology, specifically Web 2.0 tool usage in higher education in South Africa.

The initiative was investigated at a private higher education institution, Pearson Institute of Higher Education in Gauteng. The study provides empirical findings on the use of Web 2.0 tools in higher education. Thus, the purpose of this study was to investigate perceived usefulness factors influencing the usage of Web 2.0 tools in higher education. The research was conducted among academics at Pearson Institute of Higher Education.

The target population was most appropriate for this study in order to get an insight on their current level of usage of Web 2.0 tools for academic purposes as well as what factors influences academics to use Web 2.0 tools in teaching and learning. The study was conducted among 70 academics at Pearson Institute of Higher Education.

The usage of social media was adopted in education by using various educational tools when teaching. Tools that were used were YouTube, Edmodo, TedEd, Instagram and Skype. The rest of the case history will provide more details of how the social media tools were used for teaching and learning. Thus, the study will provide valuable information to academic institutions on how to enhance teaching and learning in higher education in South Africa with the use of Web 2.0 tools.

This study provided insights to stakeholders in higher education institutions on integrating Web 2.0 tools in the traditional teaching and learning environment. This will encourage collaboration amongst students as well as the sharing of information and ideas. This will help students to become actively involved in the learning process than just absorbing the information that is disseminated.

2. The challenges

A challenge experienced was that only a few social media tools were explored in teaching and learning and the study was only conducted at one higher education institution. Thus, many academics were not willing to share their opinions and experiences of Web 2.0 technology tools. In addition, the higher education institution in this study was a private institution as government institutions had been on strike and this was ongoing throughout the year. Due to this, the researcher decided to focus on a private institution's usage of Web 2.0 tools.

3. How the initiative was received by the users or participants

The academics were very open to the idea of using TedEd, Edmodo, Skype and Instagram as a teaching and learning tool. Majority of the academics make use of YouTube but were willing and interested to try different social media tools after being informed of the benefits.

4. The learning outcomes

The aim of the study was to identify innovative ways of transforming the traditional teaching approach to a more fun and informative one by adopting Web 2.0 tools in education. In order to do this, the researcher first needed to investigate educators' perception on the usefulness of Web 2.0 tools in education.

Perceived usefulness in this study is the degree to which an academic believes that using Web 2.0 tools will enhance their productivity (Davis, Bagozzi and Warshaw, 1989). Perceived usefulness of Web 2.0 tools is measured in the context of teaching and learning in academic institutions.

Perceived usefulness and the ease of use from the TAM model (Davis, 1989) have an influence on intention to use a system that ultimately affects the usage of Web 2.0 tools. Perceived ease of use is measured under the quality characteristics of Web 2.0 tools in this study.

Table 1 was used to measure the perceived usefulness against usage of Web 2.0 tools in an effort to identify significant predictors of usage.

Table 1: Cronbach Alpha for perceived usefulness

Factor	Findings	Cronbach Alpha
Perceived usefulness (PIHE) (teamwork; student-staff communication; student-staff connectivity; collaboration; content creators; use and reuse of material; active participant and online presence)	PU is a significant predictor of usage of Web 2.0 tools.	= .912

4.1 Perceived usefulness at Pearson Institute of Higher Education

The academic rank of the respondents at Pearson Institute of Higher Education was made up of 77% of lecturers, 13% senior lecturers, 9% of professors and 1% fell under the option of "Other"; this was the rank of Campus Director.

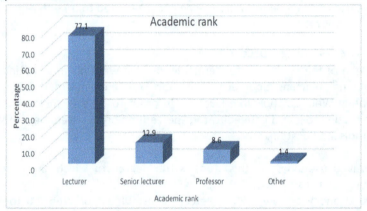

Figure 1: Academic rank of respondents at PIHE

Respondents (academics) were asked to indicate their agreement with statements regarding the usefulness/benefits of Web 2.0 tools in education. The following were the results for perceived usefulness:

4.1.1 Increased instructor- student communication and interaction

A total of 44% of respondents agreed and 23% of respondents strongly agreed that Web 2.0 tools increases interaction and communication among the instructor and students. A small proportion, 7% of respondents disagreed with the statement. The remaining 26% of respondents were neutral.

Table 2: Perceived usefulness of Web 2.0 tools at PIHE for communication and interaction

... increases interaction and communication among the instructor and students[a]

		Frequency	Percent	Valid Percent	Cumulative Percent
Valid	Disagree	5	7.1	7.1	7.1
	Neutral	18	25.7	25.7	32.9
	Agree	31	44.3	44.3	77.1
	Strongly agree	16	22.9	22.9	100.0
	Total	70	100.0	100.0	

4.1.2 *Improved student-teacher connectivity*

The findings revealed that 43% of respondents agreed and 23% of respondents strongly agreed that the usage of Web 2.0 tools helps develop a better sense of connectivity between students and teachers. 13% of respondents disagreed with the statement. The remaining 21% of respondents were neutral.

Table 3: Perceived usefulness of Web 2.0 tools at PIHE for connectivity

... helps develop a better sense of connectivity between students and teachers[a]

		Frequency	Percent	Valid Percent	Cumulative Percent
Valid	Disagree	9	12.9	12.9	12.9
	Neutral	15	21.4	21.4	34.3
	Agree	30	42.9	42.9	77.1
	Strongly agree	16	22.9	22.9	100.0
	Total	70	100.0	100.0	

5. Increased opportunity to create content

A total of 50% of respondents agreed and 21% of respondents strongly agreed that Web 2.0 tools could give students the opportunity to create content themselves instead of just listening to lectures. 13% of respondents disagreed with the statement. The remaining 16% of respondents were neutral.

Table 4: Perceived usefulness of Web 2.0 tools at PIHE for content creation

... gives students the opportunity to create content themselves instead of just listening to lectures[a]

		Frequency	Percent	Valid Percent	Cumulative Percent
Valid	Disagree	9	12.9	12.9	12.9
	Neutral	11	15.7	15.7	28.6
	Agree	35	50.0	50.0	78.6
	Strongly agree	15	21.4	21.4	100.0
	Total	70	100.0	100.0	

5.0.1 Creative use and reuse of material

A total of 40% of respondents agreed and 26% of respondents strongly agreed that the adoption of Web 2.0 tools enables academics to creatively use and reuse material in novel ways because there is not one centralised power controlling the web. A total of 9% of respondent disagreed and 10% of respondents strongly disagreed with the statement. The remaining 26% of respondents were neutral.

Table 5: Perceived usefulness of Web 2.0 tools at PIHE for using and reusing material

... allows me to creatively use and reuse material in novel ways because there is not one centralised power controlling the web[a]

		Frequency	Percent	Valid Percent	Cumulative Percent
Valid	Disagree	6	8.6	8.6	8.6
	Neutral	18	25.7	25.7	34.3
	Agree	28	40.0	40.0	74.3
	Strongly agree	18	25.7	25.7	100.0
	Total	70	100.0	100.0	

5.0.2 Shift towards active information consumption

A total of 40% of respondents agreed and 21% of respondents strongly agreed that Web 2.0 tools could change academics from a passive to an active information consumer, allowing their online voice to be part of the conversation. A small proportion, 16% of respondents disagreed with the statement. The remaining 23% of respondents were neutral.

Table 6: Perceived usefulness of Web 2.0 tools at PIHE for online presence

... changes me from a passive to an active information consumer, allowing my online voice to be part of the conversation[a]

		Frequency	Percent	Valid Percent	Cumulative Percent
Valid	Disagree	11	15.7	15.7	15.7
	Neutral	16	22.9	22.9	38.6
	Agree	28	40.0	40.0	78.6
	Strongly agree	15	21.4	21.4	100.0
	Total	70	100.0	100.0	

Based on the results obtained at Pearson Institute of Higher Education there is a significant agreement that the usage of Web 2.0 tools in education is very useful as it:

- increases interaction and communication among the instructor and students (M=3.83, SD = .868), t (69) = 7.990, p<.0005;
- helps develop a better sense of connectivity between students and teachers (M=3.76, SD = .955), t (69) = 6.636, p<.0005;
- gives students the opportunity to create content themselves instead of just listening to lectures (M=3.80, SD = .926), t (69) = 7.226, p<.0005;
- allows me to creatively use and reuse material in novel ways because there is not one centralised power controlling the web (M=3.83, SD = .916), t (69) = 7.565, p<.0005;
- changes me from a passive to an active information consumer, allowing academics' online voice to be part of the conversation (M=3.67, SD = .989), t (69) = 5.682, p<.0005.

The results are displayed below.

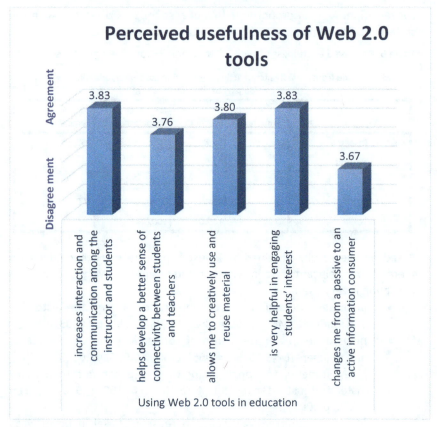

Figure 2: Perceived usefulness of using Web 2.0 tools at PIHE

Based on the findings, the following conclusions were drawn: the usage of Web 2.0 technologies at Pearson Institute of Higher Education is low and that, personal barriers was the major factor that influenced the low usage of Web 2.0 by academics.

A summary of the results of the study was that:
- A significant proportion of the sample prefer a blended teaching style (76%, $p<.0005$); and use computer applications when teaching students (94%, $p<.0005$);
- Teaching style accounts for 20.8% of the variance in USAGE ($R^2 = .208$)), $F_{(1, 125)} = 32.733$, $p<.0005$. It is a significant predictor of

usage with usage for 'blended' lecturer being significantly higher than for 'traditional' lecturers;

- Organisational sub factor of support is a significant predictor of usage;
- Perceived quality characteristics sub factor of ease of use is a significant predictor of usage of Web 2.0 tools;
- Perceived usefulness is a significant predictor of usage.

The results revealed a significant satisfaction with the use of Web 2.0 tools.

5.1 Usage of Web 2.0 applications

The purpose of this section was to determine the types of Web 2.0 applications that are used in teaching and learning. The first application to be investigated were social software applications like Facebook, flickr, etc.

A total of 54% of respondents make use of social software applications, whilst 46% of respondents do not.

Table 7: Usage of social software applications at PIHE

Social software applications like Facebook, flickr and others.[a]

		Frequency	Percent	Valid Percent	Cumulative Percent
Valid	No	32	45.7	45.7	45.7
	Yes	38	54.3	54.3	100.0
	Total	70	100.0	100.0	

5.1.1 Wikis

Wikis was another application investigated to determine the usage in education. The findings revealed that 34% of respondents make use of Wiki sites.

Table 8: Usage of Wiki sites at PIHE

Wiki sites like Wikipedia, Wiki and Javapedia and others[a]

		Frequency	Percent	Valid Percent	Cumulative Percent
Valid	No	46	65.7	65.7	65.7
	Yes	24	34.3	34.3	100.0
	Total	70	100.0	100.0	

5.1.2 *Blogging websites*
Blogging websites can also be adopted in education. Based on the results, a total of 17% of respondents make use of blogging websites.

Table 9: Usage of blogging websites at PIHE

Blogging websites like Blogger.com and Blogspot.com[a]

		Frequency	Percent	Valid Percent	Cumulative Percent
Valid	No	58	82.9	82.9	82.9
	Yes	12	17.1	17.1	100.0
	Total	70	100.0	100.0	

5.1.3 *Podcasting sites*
Thirdly, podcasting sites were investigated to determine the usage of this application in education. A total of 14% of respondents make use of podcasting sites.

Table 10: Usage of podcasting sites at PIHE

Podcasting sites like odeo.com and apple.com [a]

		Frequency	Percent	Valid Percent	Cumulative Percent
Valid	No	60	85.7	85.7	85.7
	Yes	10	14.3	14.3	100.0
	Total	70	100.0	100.0	

5.1.4 *Usage of other Web 2.0 tools*
A total of 34% of respondents stated that they use other Web 2.0 tools (besides the above mentioned applications) for educational purposes. This comprised of MyLabsPlus Pearson, Easely for assignments and virtual labs like Amrita, YouTube, and Google.

Table 11: Usage of other Web 2.0 tools at PIHE

Other[a]

		Frequency	Percent	Valid Percent	Cumulative Percent
Valid	No	46	65.7	65.7	65.7
	Yes	24	34.3	34.3	100.0
	Total	70	100.0	100.0	

A significant proportion of the sample do not make use of certain Web 2.0 tools, applications or services. This is made up of wiki sites (66%, p=.012); blogging websites (83%, p<.0005); Podcasting (86%, p<.0005) as well as other Web 2.0 tools which made up 66%, p=.012.

Figure 3 below, illustrates the findings that were discussed in Sections 4.2.1-4.2.4

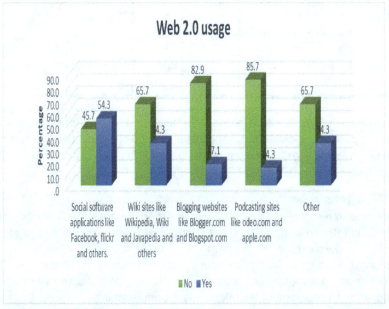

Figure 3: Web 2.0 usage at PIHE

5.1.5   Usage of Web 2.0 tools for teaching and/or for faculty use
A total of 7% of respondents stated that they use Web 2.0 tools only for teaching purposes; 9% use Web 2.0 tools only for Faculty work and the reminder 51% use Web 2.0 tools for both teaching and faculty work. A total of 33% (23 respondents out of 70) of respondents mentioned that they do not use Web 2.0 tools.

Table 12: Usage of Web 2.0 tools for teaching and/or for faculty use at PIHE

Blogs, podcasting, wikis, RSS, and Social Software for teaching and/or for faculty use

		Frequency	Percent	Valid Percent	Cumulative Percent
Valid	Teaching only	5	7.1	7.1	7.1
	Faculty work only	6	8.6	8.6	15.7
	Both teaching and faculty work	36	51.4	51.4	67.1
	Do not use	23	32.9	32.9	100.0
	Total	70	100.0	100.0	

The results of the Chi-square goodness of fit test: a significant number of the respondents indicated that they use Web 2.0 tools for teaching and for faculty use and significant number of respondents also stated they do not use Web 2.0 tools ($\chi2$ (3) = 37.771, p<.0005).

5.2   Interviews

The researcher conducted interviews in order to generalise findings from the qualitative research. Thus, the purpose of the interviews was to get a better understanding of the current level of usage of Web 2.0 tools amongst academics in higher education. In addition, to determine the themes and subthemes associated with the use Web 2.0 tools in higher education to supplement traditional classroom teaching.

The interviews were used to confirm categories/themes. Thus, the data was analysed using thematic analysis i.e. a descriptive presentation of qualitative data. This analysis enabled the researcher to categorise the data according to themes. This approach helped the researcher to move the analysis from a broad reading of the data towards discovering patterns and developing themes (Boyatzis, 1998). This approach provided a way of getting closer to the data and developing some deeper appreciation of the content by allowing patterns to be identified and commonalities, differences and relationships to be highlighted.

The qualitative data was collected by means of semi-structured in-depth interviews with academics with the purpose of gathering in-depth insights on participant attitudes, thoughts, and actions with regard to the phenomenon under study. Once the data was collected, the interview transcripts were loaded into the NVivo analysis tool in order to establish categories and themes.

5.2.1 Participants

Pearson Institute of Higher Education (PIHE) is a private higher education institution that use technology enhanced and traditional learning methods, as well as practical application, to prepare students for the technology driven and fast changing work environment of the 21st century (Pearson Institute of Higher Education, 2018). A total of eight academics participated in the interview. This is displayed in Table 13, below. The sample consisted of academics who were representative of the population of academics that use/aware of Web 2.0 tools. The interviews were about 10 minutes in length. NVivo was used to analyse the data by coding the text from the interviews.

Table 13: Interview participants at PIHE

	Disciplines	Number	Participants
PIHE	IT	3	A,B,C
	Science	3	D, E, F
	Commerce	2	G,H

5.2.2 Content category/theme A: Perceived usefulness

Theme A represents perceived usefulness. This theme is aimed at understanding educator perceptions on the usefulness/ benefits of web 2.0 tools in higher education. Table 14 will establish themes and sub themes relating to How does perceived usefulness influence the use of Web 2.0 technology tools among academics in higher education.

The count of individual occurrences of the subthemes within the perceived usefulness category/theme for Pearson Institute of Higher Education is displayed in Table 14 below. In this table, academics provided possible advantages of using Web 2.0 tools for learning when compared to the traditional lecture-based education system.

Table 14: Pearson Institute of Higher Education: perceived usefulness theme

Organising theme	Subthemes	Sources	References
	Promotes student engagement	4	5
Perceived	Flexible teaching and learning	6	6
Usefulness of Web	Facilitates content creation	2	2
2.0 tools	Access to educational resources	3	3
	Improved communication and sharing	1	1

The following were the findings related to academics' perceptions on the usefulness of Web 2.0 tools:

1. Promotes student engagement

   The data extract supporting this theme was: "Videos and online tutorials enables me to adopt a flipped classroom approach" (B2). "Students are familiar with Web 2.0 tools which encourages them to participate in class discussion" (A1); "When I use these tools, students are more eager to contribute" (G1). Students can participate in online class discussions such as blogs and forums" (D1); "Web 2.0 tools allows students to participate in online assessments and test their knowledge on the concept taught in class" (A1).

2. Flexible teaching and learning

   The data extract relating to this theme were: "Students have access to learning material outside of the classroom" (A1); "Web 2.0 tools allows students to be in control of the teaching and learning process beyond the walls of the classroom" (F3); "Teaching continues even after the student has left the class" (E2), "I use Web 2.0 tools to assist students to recap what was taught in class" (B2),"I can send learning material to my students at any time" (C3) and "the use of Web 2.0 tools provides fun ways of teaching" (G1).

3. Facilitates content creation

   Data extracts that confirmed this theme were: "Web 2.0 tools allows me to create audio and video content which helps to relay information to students" (C3) and "students can create content themselves with the use of Web 2.0 tools" (A1).

4. Access to educational resources

   Data extracts relating to his theme were: "with the use of Web 2.0 tools, students have access to a wide variety of online resources" (F3); "Web 2.0 tools allows students to gain access to online assessments and tutorials" (H2) and "students can watch video tutorials when experiencing difficulties with the content taught" (B2).

5. Improved communication and sharing
    The data extracts relating to this theme was: "I can communicate and easily share information online after class with students using Web 2.0 tools" (D1).
6. The perceived usefulness results indicated that the use of Web 2.0 tools in higher education is beneficial in teaching and learning. The majority of the academics in this study had something positive to say about Web 2.0 tools in education.
7. Based on the above findings, the researcher further explored the usage of Web 2.0 tools in education by investigating the usage of selected Web 2.0 tools amongst 100 undergraduate students at Pearson Institute of Higher Education. This was made up of 60 second year students and 40 third year students. The following tools were used in the classroom:

5.3   Skype
This tool allowed the researcher to conduct online real time classes with students off campus. This was a great tool as it transformed the teaching and learning process to take place outside of the classroom.

5.4   Instagram
Students enjoy taking photos so as part of the continuous assessment Instagram was adopted in the curriculum by creating a photo essay assignment where students had to use Instagram to take photos, upload, and add captions to a particular concept.

5.5   Edmodo
This platform was used to post notices, calendar reminders and any additional information related to the module. This was a very enjoyable tool to use for easy and effortless communication to students.

These findings revealed that students were more participative when a Web 2.0 tool was adopted in the teaching and learning process. There was also an increase in the marks obtained in the assignment that adopted blended learning with the use of a social media tool (Instagram).

6. Plans to further develop the initiative

Based on the findings of this study related to the usage of Web 2.0 tools in higher education, the following are suggestions for future research:

The study focused on factors influencing academics' usage of Web 2.0 tools from the perspective of educators and not from a student's perspective. Therefore, it would be interesting to further study factors that influences students' usage of Web 2.0 tools in education.

A future study can be conducted with educators in other universities (both private and public institutions) in different provinces of the country.

7. Conclusion

The results of this study indicated that the usage of Web 2.0 technologies is still in its infancy stages at Pearson Institute of Higher Education as the usage of Web 2.0 tools in education is not being used by all academics.

However, there was much enthusiasm amongst academics for developing the potential of Web 2.0 tools at the respective academic institution.

This study indicated that Perceived usefulness is a significant predictor of usage of Web 2.0 tools in education. An increase in the level of awareness and use of the technologies among academics for teaching and learning purposes impacts on the type of Web 2.0 tools used. The findings confirm that Web 2.0 tools are beneficial in higher education but barriers exist. This findings was useful as it helped to establish the factors that need to be present to influence the usage of Web 2.0 tools in education. There needs to be strong organisational support in order to remove these barriers.

References:

Boyatzis, R.E. 1998. Transforming qualitative information: Thematic analysis and code development. Thousand Oaks, London, & New Delhi: SAGE Publications.

Bubaš, G., Ćorić, A. and Orehovački, T. 2011. Strategies for implementation of Web 2.0 tools in academic education. Paper presented at the 17th European University Information Systems International Congress, Dublin, Ireland.

Davis, F., Bagozzi, R. and Warshaw, P. (1989). User Acceptance of Computer Technology: a comparison of two theoretical models. Management Science, 35: 982 - 1003.

Davis, F.D. 1989. Perceived Usefulness, Perceived Ease of Use, and User Acceptance of Information Technology. MIS Quarterly, 13(3): 319-340.

Yadav, A. and Patwardhan, A. 2016. Use and Impact of Web 2.0 Tools in Higher Education: A Literature Review. 218-246. [Online]. Available at:

https://www.researchgate.net/publication/306118900_Use_and_Impact_of_Web_20_To ols_in_Higher_Education_A_Literature_Review [Accessed 23 July 2018].

Author Biography

Kebashnee Moodley is an academic at Pearson Institute of Higher Education (Gauteng) in South Africa. She has 10 years of experience in higher education. Kebashnee has a Masters and Honours degree in Information systems and technology and is passionate about implementing technology in education.

Kebashnee Moodley

Using a WhatsApp Group Chat (WGC) for staff Development

Granny Setswe, Maria Madiope and Mpine Makoe
University of South Africa
magrans27@gmail.com
Madiom@unisa.ac.za
Qakisme@unisa.ac.za

Abstract: Twenty-first century academics work flexible hours and would prefer to have access to training anytime and anywhere. Mobile Learning is learning that takes place through social and content interaction using personal electronic devices. Academic staff development is mainly conducted via workshops – a solution not suited to this group as they tend to work flexible hours. Using mobile devices is beneficial as this allows academics to access training wherever they may be. The aim of this study was to explore the use of a WhatsApp Group Chat (WGC) for staff development using an intervention delivered via WGC. The intervention explored the use of the WGC as a learning platform for staff development. This is a qualitative study which used participants' WGC trail messages to collect data. The design-based research model was used with the Analysis, Design, Development, Implementation and Evaluation (ADDIE) model to develop the intervention. A WGC was created by a Group Administrator (GA) who added members using their phone numbers. Two WGCs were created, comprising ten academics and three instructional designers. Intervention activities were conducted over four weeks and on different topics. Participants completed all units and participated in group discussions to complete their training. At the end of training period, the GA downloaded full transcripts of all chats. Each WGC transcript was qualitatively analysed and the results were grouped according to common themes using thematic content analysis. Qualitative analysis of the WGC transcripts showed that the GA provided instructions, outcomes, training structure and information on how to engage in discussions. The training intervention showed that WGC was well received as a platform for professional development. However, implementation of this intervention showed problems of compatibility and accessibility of content via mobile devices as participants used their own devices. The findings of the study revealed that the use of WGC is effective for staff development as it is flexible and inclusive.

1. Introduction

The specific objective of the social media initiative was to explore the use of mobile learning technologies for the professional development of academics at a University of Technology (UoT). In order to attain the aim of this study, the following sub questions are addressed:

- To what extent would it be feasible to use mobile learning technology to deliver training to academics within a University of Technology?
- What learning design principles best support mobile learning technologies for the professional development of academics?
- Which mobile learning design frameworks can be used for training and learning solutions?

This study involved the empowerment of academics towards integrating mobile learning into teaching and learning.

2. Literature Review

Social networks have become an integral part of student social life (Deng & Tavares, 2013). The presence of positive and negative sides of social networks does not change the fact that these tools are rapidly becoming popular, gaining an important place in our lives, and starting to take their place in education. (Cetinkaya, 2017).

WhatsApp Messenger platform is a free mobile messaging available for smartphones and Android which allows users to exchange messages and receive messages, without having to pay short message service (SMS) charges. According to Minhas et al (2016), people nowadays use WhatsApp Messenger frequently to remain in touch with friends and family. This platform connects users across all cellular network service providers and mobile devices within a closed group, allowing them to send messages, photos, images, video, calls, documents and audio media as well to share their location. The WhatsApp Group Chat feature allows group administrator creates a group that users can access only by invitation of the administrator then users post messages to the group. Ngaleka and Uys (2013) reported that WhatsApp can be used to facilitate mobile learning.

Tang and Hew (2017) reported that WhatsApp has been used in different academic disciplines to support students' learning. WhatsApp can be used in higher education in a number of ways to achieve different educational goals (Gasaymeh, 2017).

Gachago, Strydom, Hanekom, Simons, and Walters (2015) argue that WhatsApp can be used in higher education to create immediate connections, encourage reflection, and facilitate coordination in informal and formal learning. Chipunza (2013) found that WhatsApp was a useful electronic tool to facilitate information sharing among university students on a range of subjects related to the courses that they were studying.

Tarighat and Khodabakhsh (2016) found that WhatsApp can be useful in language assessment.

When such social networks are designed in accordance with the needs of science and information, it is alleged that they have the potential to bring about revolutionary changes (Zaidieh, 2012), and their influence on the educational environment is increasing rapidly every day, especially with the help of the internet-supported mobile technologies. (Cetinkaya, 2017).

Rambe and Bere ((2013) says that WhatsApp Messenger was adopted to allow for synchronous and asynchronous interaction and it could be useful to create alternative dialogic spaces for student collaborative engagements in informal contexts, which can gainfully transform teaching. The USAID-funded Knowledge for Health (K4Health) Project in 2016 tested the WhatsApp Messenger platform as a mode to deliver a seven-week training programme on healthy timing and spacing of pregnancy (HTSP), delivering professional development training content to Kenyan health workers and promoting knowledge exchange and discussion. The overall purpose of K4Health's WhatsApp HTSP training activity was to test the acceptability and feasibility of the WhatsApp Group Chat feature as a learning platform.

The findings from this training activity reveal that WhatsApp is well received as a platform for continuing professional development. However, implementation of this activity also led to a number of lessons being learned around training setup, facilitation, and active participation.

This current study explores the use of WhatsApp Group Chat as an effective and affordable platform for professional development.

Rutherford (2010) in his study expresses that social media offers teachers an encouraging, participatory, practical, collaborative and dynamic environment and help teachers' professional development in the fields such as pedagogical content knowledge and field knowledge.

The study on the role of WhatsApp Messenger in the Laboratory Management System (Dorwal et al, 2016) looked at the impact of using the WhatsApp messenger service in the laboratory management system, by forming multiple groups of the various subsections of the laboratory. In this study, total of 35 members used this service for a period of 3 months (from August to October 2014) and their response was taken on a scale of 1 to 10.

A total of thirty five (35) laboratory personnel, who included both the scientific and medical staff, were part of the study belonging to various subsections of the Department of Pathology and Laboratory Medicine at a hospital. Only the lab workers who had access to smart phone and had the WhatsApp application in their smart phones were included in the study.

There was significant improvement in the communication in the form of sharing photographic evidence, information about accidents, critical alerts, duty rosters, academic activities and getting directives from seniors.

There was also some increase in the load of adding information to the application and disturbance in the routine activities; but the benefits far outweighed the minor hassles. A questionnaire was prepared that included various questions on the expected outcome of the use of WhatsApp messenger service. The results of the questions from the 35 participants were recorded in a MS-Excel sheet and were analysed using paired student t-test to compare the mean of the results. Of the total of 12 positive questions that were put-forth, eight (8) were positive questions while four (4) were negative questions. Dorwal et al, (2016) study proves that the judicious use of social media (WhatsApp messenger in this case) can significantly aid in improving communication across the laboratory/ diagnostic services, thereby ensuring timely intervention/ action (where required), and enabling information sharing amongst partners and stake-holders, which ultimately translates in improved patient care and quality of healthcare service.

In a study by Cansoy (2017), kinds of shares made by science teachers in a WhatsApp group as an online community of practice to support professional development were examined. In this study the netnographic research method was used in which messages shared by 12 science teachers who worked at a private school between the years 2015-2016, in the WhatsApp group were examined. The teachers' shares in the WhatsApp group were collected under four main themes described as the shares for field knowledge, pedagogical content knowledge, teaching practices in school and emotional support. In teachers' shares for field knowledge in the WhatsApp group, they discussed the principles and concepts within the context of the questions asked during the lesson. In other words, teachers examined a science question mutually and deeply.

This allowed teachers the opportunity to think deeply about principles and concepts. In their shares, teachers tried to create appropriate answers to the subjects in different disciplines of science with a multiple viewpoint. In addition to these, they shared computer software, useful web pages, photographs and videos related to the subject area that they can use during their lessons. With these shares, teachers also encouraged each other to use technology effectively.

From this point of view, it can be said that teachers made efforts to be able to use and increase the field information as required by means of their shares in WhatsApp groups. On the other side, it can be said that the other teachers in the group also increased their knowledge by following the discussions in the group. Cansoy (2017) concluded that online communities of practice provide a social environment in which professional development of teachers is supported. The information sharing is made and that different opinions are discussed in virtual communities of practice among teachers. (Alakurt and Keser, 2014).

Marcia and Garcia, 2016 stated that teachers' participation in online communities of practice will encourage them to experience new methodologies, acquire new resources and think about educational theories.

This study indicates that the online community of practice among group of teachers on WhatsApp, supports the professional development of teachers.

It further stated that use of social media tools among teachers helps teachers to use knowledge by reinterpreting it (Cranefield & Yoong, 2009). Also these groups provide cooperation and social support enabling teachers to think about different practices (Smith Risser, 2013). According to Barhoumi (2015) the attitudes of students toward the use of WhatsApp mobile learning activities show that the learning process facilitates learning, helps users find solutions to their learning difficulties, easily construct and share knowledge, and supports research into useful information for learning. The learning process which integrates WhatsApp mobile learning activities is more effective for learning and teaching than face to face learning process.

WhatsApp mobile learning activities can be powerful and effective tools for students. (Barhoumi, 2015).

3. The Intervention

The learning intervention forming part of this study was implemented with academics and learning and development specialists at a University of Technology. The system for the delivery of the intervention was the WhatsApp platform used on a mobile phone or laptop. The intervention itself was created in the PowerPoint presentation software. Consent to participate in the study was obtained from thirteen academics and instructional designers. Two WhatsApp Group Chats were created on the WhatsApp platform and all participants were invited to the relevant Chat; one for academics and the other for instructional designers.

Twelve participants accepted the invitation to participate. The researcher posted an introduction and information about the discussion of the intervention and encouraged collaboration between users. The researcher recorded a welcome message and posted it to the Group Chat. The intervention activities for the WhatsApp Group Chats were conducted over four (4) consecutive weeks and covered different topics. Week 1 dealt with orientation to the learning intervention and the researcher posted unit one and its associated activities to the groups. Most participants checked in to the Group Chat and started to participate in unit one and its activities. The participation was vibrant and the researcher encouraged more participation from those whose initial participation was limited. At the end of the week, the researcher closed the discussion and prepared participants for the next activity. Week 2 dealt with learning unit

46

navigation and netiquette guidelines. The researcher posted the unit and its associated activities to the groups and included information about buttons that participants could use to navigate and guidelines on how to conduct themselves during the online chats. To assess understanding of this content, participants responded to an online quiz sent in through Google forms. They obtained the results of the quiz instantly. The researcher then posted questions to the chat concerning the unit. At the end of the week, participants shared their reflections on the unit. Participants said that they had performed well on the quiz. They had learned how to use navigation buttons and also learnt a lot concerning how to conduct themselves when they participate in Group Chats. Week dealt with the learning content and activities about use of mobile learning and technologies employed in academic development. The researcher posted the learning content via WhatsApp, with video content included so as to accommodate all learning styles. Participants went through the learning content and then responded to the questions posted by the researcher.

Participants reported that they had learnt about mobile learning and that the content was precise and to the point. Week 4 served as a wrap up of what had gone before. The unit distributed was a summary of the previous three units and it served to close up the intervention. Participants shared their overall reflections and experience before they exited the group. The general feeling was that they had needed this interaction and that they had enjoyed it. However, the timing was not favourable as the intervention coincided with the period in which participants had to mark examinations. Screen shots of the learning intervention used for this study are presented below.

For the purposes of this paper, only two screen shots (title slide and table of contents slides) will be used.

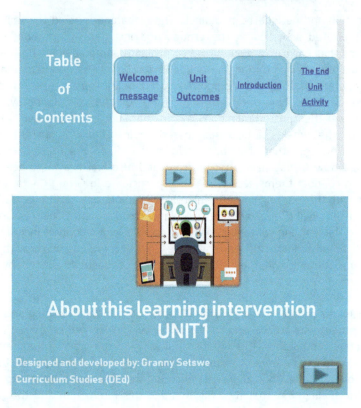

Figure 1: The Infrastructure

4. Role of Facilitator

The researcher served as WhatsApp Group administrator for the two groups of participants (academics and instructional designers) taking part in the study. In this role, the administrator promoted knowledge exchange and learning around the different topics posted to each group. The researcher/administrator's responsibilities included the following:

- Inviting and adding group members to their respective groups
- Encouraging members to actively participate on WhatsApp group chats
- Posting all the units and their activities to all participants
- Providing group members with technical support in the use of WhatsApp

- Monitoring the activity within the groups – with particular reference to the appropriateness and accuracy of posts

5. Mobile Learning Intervention Plan

The training intervention was executed as follows:

Table 1: Implementation plan

ACTIVITY	TIMEFRAME
Request permission from the HOD to conduct research at the sampled department	End of Sep 2018
Notification to the participants and WhatsApp group chat creation	Oct 2018
Intervention activities and topics: This will be conducted in four consecutive weeks Week 1: About the learning intervention: Getting started unit/orientation unit to guide participants Know your participants survey Check-ins of the participants and the researcher WhatsApp Discussions: Participant engagement End of week activity (Assessment activity)	29 Oct- 2 Nov 2018
Week 2: Navigation and netiquette guidelines WhatsApp Discussions: Learning context End of week activity (Reflection and experiences)	5 - 9 Nov 2018
Week 3: Learning content and activities WhatsApp Discussions: Seek to challenge participants and provide them with practice End of week activity (Reflection and experiences)	11 -16 Nov 2018
Week 4: Wrap Up (End of the course) WhatsApp Discussions: Feedback about the learning experiences and suitability for implementation of the learning intervention Final remarks	19- 30 Nov 2018

6. Methodology

This was a qualitative study undertaken using the Design-Based Research (DRB) model along with the Analysis, Design, Development, Implementation and Evaluation (ADDIE) model to develop the intervention. DRB is aligned to the various ADDIE phases and both start with an analysis phase in order to explore the educational problem. Both are also theory-driven, interactive and iterative, and are, by design, conducted in real-world settings while the researcher works collaboratively with the participants. ADDIE and DRB both use learning design principles to develop a learning intervention. The use of WhatsApp Group Chat for data collection occurred in phase 4 of the ADDIE model at which time the researcher collected data via WhatsApp Group Chat with academics and instructional designers at a University of Technology. The researcher obtained consent from those participants who would form part of the group.

Thereafter, the researcher coordinated, participants' collaboration and gave feedback during the discussion sessions. Qualitative data was collected through individual interviews and via WhatsApp Group Chat (WGC) trail messages with academics and instructional designers. Collected data from all interviews were recorded to audio while WGC were exported and saved for analysis. The audio data was transcribed and typed into a Word document before analysis. Thematic analysis was used to analyse data collected so as to be able to identify, analyse and report patterns (themes) within data.

6.1　The challenges; how the initiative was received by users or participants; and learning outcomes

The main challenges encountered were the compatibility and accessibility of content via mobile devices. The timing was not favourable as the intervention coincided with the period in which participants had to mark examinations. The challenges experienced arose due to participants using their own devices which were not standardised with the device used by the researcher and also due to the struggles experienced by some participants in using basic technology. The challenges were overcome when the researcher emailed the intervention to be accessed through the computer. The chats mainly happened in the evenings when most academics were not marking examinations. The initiative was received with enthusiasm with participants reporting that they felt they needed this interaction and saying that they enjoyed it. They also said that the learning unit is straight forward and user friendly. Participants felt they needed this interaction and said they enjoyed it. However, the timing was not favourable as the research took place at a time when they were marking examination scripts. The findings of the study revealed that WGC as a social media is effective for staff development as it is flexible and inclusive. Barhoumic (2015) found that the use of WhatsApp to facilitate blended learning had a positive and significant impact on students' learning performance and their attitudes toward blended learning.

Bansal and Joshi (2014) examined the experiences of students at a college of education with WhatsApp mobile learning and found that the use of

WhatsApp increased these students' social interactivity with each other and with the instructor, and that this facilitated collaborative learning. In addition, the authors found that students had positive attitudes toward the use of WhatsApp in their leaning. The learning outcome of using WhatsApp Group Chat to implement a mobile learning intervention among academics was successfully achieved. At the end of intervention session, participants completed the mobile learning design evaluation checklist to provide their input about the learning intervention. WhatsApp Group Chat as a data collection method was deemed successful in measuring the implementation of the mobile learning intervention. At the beginning of the WhatsApp Group Chat session, I send a survey 'Know your target audience' so the results were:

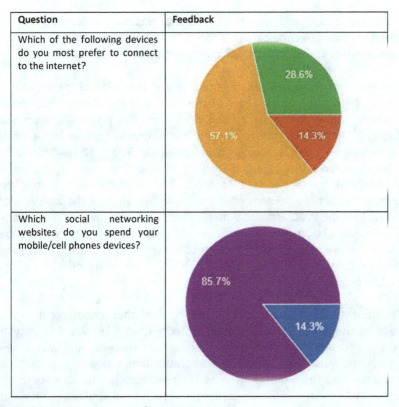

Figure 2: Know your target audience survey

7. Future Plans
The researcher used the data as interpreted in order to refine, modify the intervention, add gaps that learning design required, made changes on the look and feel to enhance the intervention for future use.This research project was successful in using a WhatsApp Group Chat to implement a mobile learning intervention among academics at a university. The overall participation in the four units was vibrant and the researcher encouraged more participation from those who, initially, were less keen to participate.

The future plan is to design and develop a generic intervention that employs best design principles supporting mobile technologies.

8. Conclusion
The study in which the WhatApp Group Chat was used, explored the use of mobile learning technologies for the development of staff. This involved empowerment of academics using intervention delivered via WhatsApp.

The intervention tested the acceptability and feasibility of the WhatsApp Group Chat feature as a learning platform for staff development training to promote knowledge exchange and discussion. This research project was successful in using a WhatsApp Group Chat to implement a mobile learning intervention among academics at a university. The features offered by WhatsApp have the potential to bring solutions to training challenges experienced in face-to-face learning. The final analysis is not yet completed, but the findings after the implementation of the intervention reveal that the WGC as a social media platform is effective for professional development because it is flexible and inclusive. The findings further show that there are motivators for using mobile technology for the professional development of academics as well as barriers to the introduction of the mobile technology.

The motivators that participants identified were that the intervention was easy to use, user friendly, met expectations, was simple, was easy to access and efficient, catered for 21st century students and was a new trend of learning. WhatsApp is a collaborative tool, interactive, instant and attractive and the benefits were expressed concisely. The barriers to the use of WGC for the professional development of academics were the lack of data and network, the diverse socio-economic backgrounds and lack of technological knowledge of participants, the functionalities of mobile devices for navigation that did not work and the problems with technology, etc. Thus far, the findings of the study revealed that WGC as a social media is effective for academic development of staff and that the use of the WGC was a positive experience to support the professional development of the academics at the UoT.

The learning outcome of using WhatsApp Group Chat to implement a mobile learning intervention among academics was successfully achieved.

References

Alakurt, T., and Keser, H. (2014). Sanal uygulama topluluğu üyelerinin bilgi paylaşımı davranışlarının incelenmesi.İlköğretim Online, 13(4), 1331-1351.

Bansal, T., and Joshi, D. (2014). A study of students experiences of WhatsApp mobile learning. Global Journal of Human-Social Science Research, 14(4).

Barhoumi, C. (2015) The Effectiveness of WhatsApp Mobile Learning Activities Guided by Activity Theory on Students' Knowledge Management. Contemporary Educational Technology, 6(3), 221-238

Cansoy, R., (2017). Teachers' Professional Development: The Case of WhatsApp. Journal of Education and Learning, 6(4), pp.285-293. https://doi.org/10.1108/14684520910951203

Chipunza, P. R. C. (2013) Using mobile devices to leverage student access to collaboratively generated resources: A case of WhatsApp instant messaging at a South African University.

Deng, L. and Tavares, N. (2013). From Moodle to Facebook: Exploring students' motivation and experiences in online communities. Computers & Education, 68,167–176. Retrieved from http://www.journals.elsevier.com/computers-and-education/

Dorwal, P., Sachdev, R., Gautam, D., Jain, D., Sharma, P., Tiwari, A.K. and Raina, V., (2016) Role of WhatsApp messenger in the laboratory management system: a boon to communication. Journal of medical systems, 40(1), p.14.

Gasaymeh, A.M.M., (2017) University students' use of WhatsApp and their perceptions regarding its possible integration into their education. Global Journal of Computer Science and Technology.

Gachago, D., Strydom, S., Hanekom, P., Simons, S., and Walters, S. (2015) Crossing boundaries: lecturers' perspectives on the use of WhatsApp to support teaching and learning in higher education. Progressio, 37(1), 172-187.

Macià, M., and García, I. (2016). Informal online communities and networks as a source of teacher professional development: A review. Teaching and Teacher Education, 55, 291-307.

https://doi.org/10.1016/j.tate.2016.01.021

Minhas, S., Ahmed, M. and Ullah, Q.F., 2016. Usage of WhatsApp: A Study of University of Peshawar, Pakistan. International Journal of Humanities and Social Science Invention, 5(7), pp.71-73.

Ngaleka, A., and Uys, W. (2013, June). M-learning with WhatsApp: A conversation analysis. Academic Conferences International Limited.

Rambe, P., and Bere, A., 2013. Using mobile instant messaging to leverage learner participation and transform pedagogy at a South African University of Technology. British Journal of Educational Technology, 44(4), pp.544-561.

Rutherford, C. (2010) Facebook as a source of informal teacher professional development. In Education, 16(1), 60-74.

Smith Risser, H. (2013) Virtual induction: A novice teacher's use of twitter to form an informal mentoring network. Teaching and Teacher Education, 35(1), 25-33. https://doi.org/10.1016/j.tate.2013.05.001

Tang, Y., and Hew, K. F. (2017). Is mobile instant messaging (MIM) useful in education? Examining its technological, pedagogical, and social affordances. Educational Research Review. Retrieved June 8, 2017, from http://www.science direct.com/science/article/pii/S0747563216305039 46.

Tarighat, S., and Khodabakhsh, S. (2016) Mobile-assisted language assessment: Assessing speaking. Computers in Human Behavior.

Zaidieh, A. J. Y. (2012) The use of social networking in education: challenges and opportunities. World of Computer Science and Information Technology Journal (WCSIT), 2(1), 18-21.

Author Biography

Granny Setswe is a PhD student at University of South Africa. She obtained her Master's degree in 2005 in Computer Based Education. She is an experienced Instructional Designer and Curriculum Designer in a Learning and Development environment. Her research is in the area of using mobile technology for professional development.

The Social Mixer for a Class Apart

Dr. Nitin Varma[1] and Dr. Piotr Wisniewski[2]
[1]**Chitkara University, Punjab – India**
[2]**Chartered MCSI Associate Professor, Institute of Finance, Warsaw School of Economics, Poland**
nitin.varma@chitkara.edu.in
piotr.wisniewski@sgh.waw.pl

Abstract: A graduate class, especially in developing countries such as India or Poland, can often comprise diversity sui generis. Students need to reframe their thoughts in "English", at best their lingua franca – given rising linguistic pluralism in increasingly globalized academic settings. Some students grew up as "unequals" in discussions; some students question the very processes and intent of "questioning" itself while others hold that class participation (i.e. asking or answering) makes them come across as less "smart". Thus, for varying reasons, many students will fail to question, answer or take class discussions seriously. Consequently, private visits to faculty with repetitive sets of questions and similar discussions engender information chaos and time inefficiencies. Thus, low-quality classroom interactions and subpar knowledge diffusion ensure foundational knowledge of students is ridden with uncertainties. Yes, there is a desire for a propitious and functional learning environment, that may address the aforesaid. This desire often gets swept under the carpet, in classrooms hosting multinational students and in several countries on the culture gradient. Our social media initiative aimed, to begin with, at ~12000 students of a University and concept-tested in front of 80 stakeholders, provides a conducive environment for students to freely express what is termed "knowledge-structured feedback" with respect to course outlines, including in discreet mode. It provides students with an ongoing opportunity for wider engagement at four levels: class (section), subject, department and community – with learning assistance options, response cruise control and in-built response tracking. It creates an enabling self-sustaining structured environment that incentivizes learning focus by helping minimize "the negative effects of personalities on learning, without diminishing the persons involved", thus significantly enhancing learning interactions, certainties & efficiencies through continuous conversion of course outline feedback to knowledge sharing outcomes. Besides, it may promote cost-efficiencies, vital for internationally competitive learning environment.

1. Introduction to the specific objectives of the Case

1.1   Background

The KASA model (Bennett and Rockwell 1995) emphasized knowledge, attitudes, skills and aspirations are the new fuel that drive individuals and our collective future from the perspective of long-term impact of education. Also, the advent of information age, knowledge economy and proliferation of facilities for formal education have attracted more knowledge seekers and made possible a far bigger and far more diverse student base than ever, throughout various levels of education.

The industrial revolutions sweeping the West have ensured percolation of a much more homogeneous culture to the student level as well. However, outside those countries - in a big majority of this world, natural diversity and a lack of common ethos have ensured expectations and behaviors vary from one extreme to the other.

Yet, globalization of education opportunities has ensured that diversity of expectations and behaviors has crossed boundaries and can also be expected in fairly advanced countries, at least in their international classrooms. This expectation of diversity is reflected amply through dedicated declarations of care for diversity on the websites of most universities in developed countries, as, for example - an online search with the terms "diversity, classroom, university" rapidly shows. It is interesting to note though, in some countries, classroom diversity is increasing tremendously even at the school level (Society for Diversity America 2017).

Thus, students come to university classroom with different backgrounds, sets of experiences, cultural contexts, and world views – this can result in several diversity problem scenarios (Yale 2019).

Not only that, diversity in classrooms may be expected to grow further, not only in physical classrooms, but also as offline-online classrooms become more common.

While diversity does add richness and has its own merits, there are aspects of this diversity that can affect knowledge diffusion processes, academic performance and education outcomes (Garibay 2015).

For example, diversity can affect class participation - a key academic process that in turn affects knowledge diffusion, academic performance and overall education outcomes.

Even in routine classrooms, class participation is a challenge to manage. Diversity adds multiple dimensions and it makes it even more complex.

For example, many students come from cultures where questioning was never a technique for learning, but blind followership was. These students are likely to lie low with their questions – and therefore, knowledge gaps are likely to persist, especially with the speed of delivery expected in competitive classrooms.

There are other students, who grew up believing that raising questions was equivalent to challenging authority. Many such students, in turn, silently accept this as a value, and they, in turn start looking at anyone questioning them – as a challenge to their authority. Such students are less likely to view favorably academic questioning by even faculty.

There are students who grew up in a way that confuses politeness and respect with raising questions to the faculty. Such students can accept whatever knowledge they are served, without having the motive to expanding its base through questioning and discussion.

For many students coming from a non-English speaking culture, even if they are willing to participate in class discussions, a conversation in English still requires a lot of effort and mental calculations. Such students can avoid class discussions.

Then, there are other students, that despite all else being favorable – just believe that class participation is a sign of desperation to get noticed or to provide a glimpse of one's intellect, that class participation will make them look "less smart".

Some young faculty can also be afflicted by similar aspects of their personalities - they too were students till yesterday! Their personalities can also impact class participation (Bart, 2016).

As an end result, while class discussions end up less rich, interactive and stimulating, students often seek private placement of their queries – via often repetitive private discussions with faculty. The lack of effective learning and time inefficiencies mean knowledge diffusion, academic performance and overall education outcomes are severely affected. These continue to pose unresolved challenges to educational and knowledge delivery infrastructure and environment also.

1.1.1 Our Solution

The app offers what it calls a "knowledge structured feedback" environment for class participation by seeking to minimize the undesirable effects of personalities on class discussions. It offers features that enforce behaviors conducive to productive and efficient class participation – even anonymous mode, though not untraceable. Thus, it brings a personality of its own – that is designed in a way to enhance class participation while minimizing side effects.

Designed with the aim of uncovering and addressing knowledge gaps, "knowledge structured feedback" (or simply "feedback") is contextual and can have two components:
1. The objective component: this component is feedback about the student's understanding and grasp on each item of the course outline and is on a pre-determined standardized scale
2. The subjective component: may have student comments or may provide additional details about the objective component itself, or it may even take the form of questions (called "a requested question or request") that solicit clarification or expand the scope of discussion

2. The Infrastructure (i.e. systems, exercises, or hardware, software if any)

First, it is important to develop an understanding of the new class participation opportunity accorded by this app, so this example below may be considered.

The overall student population in Semester 5 is divided into 8 classes– 5A, 5B … 5H. Each class has a faculty member specifically assigned for teaching a common subject, say Python Programming Fundamentals.

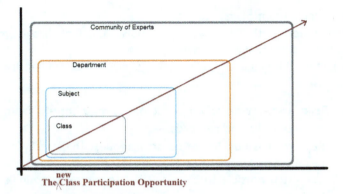

Community of Experts

Department

Subject

Class

new
The Class Participation Opportunity

Figure 1: The New Class Participation Opportunity

The Department of Computer Science and Engineering(DCSE) also has several faculty members that possess Python Programming capabilities, but these faculty are not at present involved in teaching any of the sections 5A, 5B …. 5H, because, by rotation or for other reasons- they are teaching some other subjects to even other sections.

Beyond the DCSE, there is a Community of Experts (CoE) in Python. The University has a number of Schools that utilize Python and therefore these schools often have their own exclusive faculty –at times full-time but also quite often visiting- that specializes in Python, e.g. the School of Healthcare has Healthcare Analytics and hence this school has their own exclusive Python faculty.

The App Architecture comprises the following:
Inbuilt roles: such as the Departmental Head, the overall Course Co-ordinator, Faculty-in-charge of a particular class, students, all faculty within the Department and experts on the subject available even in other departments of the University.

Key features:
1. Autopilot: the system is designed to enable a certain degree of automatic flow of information across levels

2. Automatic accelerator: through context-awareness, the system can automatically accelerate requests

3. Manual controllers:

- Accelerator – this is the manual override that allows manual acceleration of requests
- Rejector- this is the manual rejection override that can be triggered if necessary

2.1 Risks and Rewards: all participants may benefit from a fair share of risks and rewards

- Report: it is possible to report a request that totally does not belong there
- Like: it is possible to offer a "Like" to a request to indicate its usefulness
- Points: it is possible for those creating or fulfilling legitimate requests to rightfully and automatically gain participation points
- Outside comfort zone: it allows creation of requests that expand the knowledge debate to beyond syllabus

2.2 Supervisor analytics and dashboards

1. Situational deployment: the app can be used in a number of situations to provide new offerings:

- To measure effectiveness of delivery against a course outline
- For identification of knowledge gaps against a course outline
- For delivering on identified knowledge gaps against a course outline
- For identification of specific knowledge requirements, e.g. placements or trainings
- To provide extended internship support

2.3 Modes of support that can be requested:

- Special Fill-in Lecture
- Expert Lecture
- Remote support
- Specially designed training module
- Additional self-help material – online links and tutorials

At present, this is a locally available app that could be made public for wider availability to a more distributed audience, as necessary.

3. The Challenges (how and when they were encountered, how they were overcome)

The app faced people and process challenges.

For example, even though a standardized course outline was available, it needed to be prepared in such a way that it would be machine- friendly. Since every faculty member is responsible for preparing the desired course outline for their subject, when it comes to uploading the course outline - a new role had to be trained, for final quality control. Then, it required testing by the students to make sure no topic in the course outline was left outside the purview of being machine searchable.

The need for this app, at the time of conception, was itself debated. The HOD and many others at the time of conception stated that existing feedback mechanisms were delivering the feedback required about faculty suitability and effectiveness for a particular course. Upon learning more about the app, they were satisfied that current feedback mechanisms were snapshot approaches that often sought to assess faculty attributes primarily – to serve as faculty feedback rather than serving as feedback towards discovering knowledge gaps in context of the designed course.

The head of placement also initially expressed doubts that the app would be able to provide any actionable insights that could help students succeed in placement interviews. However, after a discussion about the feedback collected from students about their technical knowledge gaps post-placement process, the placement head also agreed the app had potential to uncover new insights through analysis of collected information.

The students initially perceived this as an exercise to make them work more on feedback with little benefit for them and felt the app was a bit intrusive as it sought them to spell out their doubts. With considerable explanation, students started perceiving this app would provide them the opportunity to provide feedback about knowledge gaps measured against the designed course outline for the first time. The students felt that they would be able to now, with precision, talk about their personalized course input requirements, and even incognito – to a certain degree.

The few faculty members surveyed were not so sure about this app in the beginning – because this app seemed like one more attempt to collect highly personalized feedback in disguise, albeit of continuous nature. It took some time for the app-preview faculty to realize that this app was seeking exactly the opposite – by delinking personalities of all concerned, from the feedback. Then, majority of the faculty members opened up to considering the app favorably. There still were some reservations about the risks and rewards, but even those, after efficiencies and in-built transparency were explained, were alleviated.

A key challenge related to the design of the app – making feedback visible at progressive levels in auto-pilot mode yet tracking the responses in full public view. That initially made many uncomfortable, however, when it became clear that there were inherent protections against biased behaviors, those concerns were alleviated.

4. User Test (how the initiative was received by the users or participants)

The concept was showcased to stakeholders – including students, via a presentation with a live demo. This was an open event in the University that was announced a week in advance. All students and faculty from various departments were invited. About 80 participants reviewed the presentation and the demo. These consisted 10 faculty members – senior and junior, including a representative deputed by the top management of the University.

All of those present expect to use the app, when made available formally. Here are some of the findings from the evaluation of this App:
1. Simple to use, also mobile friendly
2. Focus is on finding knowledge gaps, not on finding faults with students or faculty
3. Effective in searching and presenting related feedback / questions
4. It encourages class participation on both ends - by students and faculty
5. Many expert forums are intimidating for fresh students, here students can also choose a dynamic anonymous mode, though all identities are traceable by the admin
6. It saves a lot of time and energies spent on queries and discussions that can be held in the common
7. The app provides feed-back near real-time, that also can be useful in certain situations

8. The app provides relevant information that can help identify intervention opportunities towards modification of knowledge delivery processes and elimination of knowledge gaps

5. Learning Outcomes (What was achieved and how the outcomes were measured/evaluated)

The app provides numerous benefits and in several ways. Compared to existing snapshot approaches, this app provides a continuous mechanism for feedback and engagement.

Managing Requests: whenever there is a knowledge gap, a request may be raised by one or more students so that the knowledge gap may be filled by a contributor. The app provides numerous features and benefits for managing requests:

1. The app provides a social mixer for class participation – also in anonymous mode – so that students can take advantage of the "knowledge structured feedback" at their own convenience
2. This has enabled a lot more students to actively participate in the "class" for discussions and clearing of doubts
3. Since contributors also can earn credits for their participation, there is a sense of "not doing it for free" that additionally drives enthusiasm
4. Also, a lot more contributors can participate on a routine basis, because now the requests raised gain much higher exposure and visibility – which extends beyond the typical classroom in which a request was raised
5. Time and resources locked in answering repetitive requests are now available for other gainful activities
6. The significantly broader exposure to requests enables participation of experts even beyond the department, that would otherwise lie in a state of disconnect as islands of expertise

Analytics Insights for continuous improvement of delivery: while so far feedback collected through paper forms provided a snapshot in time, this app provides a highly granular continuous view. It offers several benefits for learning analytics insights about knowledge gaps as these happen:

- It accords granular visibility into student comfort with a topic, a chapter or part of a course

- Information gained could even be combined with student background to answer questions that currently go unanswered, using the framework: who, what, when, where, why, how, how often, i.e.

1. Who (which student coming from a certain background) is likely to face a challenge with a specific topic or chapter or part of the course?
2. What challenges are students likely to face?

5.1 Which topics overall, are likely to be perceived as tough

1. Which chapters within each part can be perceived as tough?
2. Which topics within which chapters can be perceived as tough
3. Which topics within what chapters in what part of the subject can be perceived as tough

5.2 When do the students perceive these topics as tough?

1. When are these knowledge gaps discernible?
2. When this subject was taught before a foundational subject X had been taught?
3. What can be the impact of these knowledge gaps on subjects taught later?

5.3 Where

1. For example, indicates which class or section
2. Which specific university campus or location or group – physical or virtual
3. In interviews of which organizations?

5.4 Why

1. Helps learn contributing factors
2. Contributing factors may be specific or local

5.5 How do these knowledge gaps manifest for students?

1. What do the students do, because of these difficulties
2. Is there an association between the perceived difficulties and subsequent student academic choices - regarding subjects, specializations, internships or placements?
3. What is the impact of perceived difficulties on the overall graduation?

4. What is the impact of perceived difficulties during the graduation on the career choices made by a student?
5. What is the lifelong impact?

5.6   How often

1. Is a topic always, or sometimes, or randomly, or just a few times – cited as difficult?
2. Does a student that comes from a background, culture or any such broader classification variable – cite common or similar difficulties?
3. Do faculty with certain backgrounds need deeper engagement on certain topics or with certain students?
4. How often did interventions become mandatory for a given batch throughout their progression in graduation?

Here are a few key snapshots of the application:

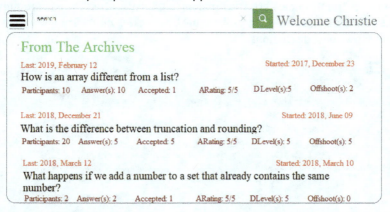

Figure 2: From the Archives

The login can be configured to bring a logged-in student at Figure 2 above. It shows past requests from the archives and a search option.

A student must begin by starting a search – existing responses(answers) are accorded a priority over ability to create new request directly. This ensures students develop a mindset of reading and reviewing the existing knowledge base.

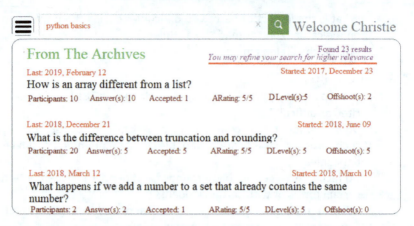

Figure 3: Search shows relevant results

Say a student searches for "Python Basics" as in Figure 3. All related requests from the past are shown along with key metrics for each request. A student may review each past request by clicking on it. The div expands and shows past discussions.

Figure 4: Search returns no results

Figure 4 shows a case in which the search returns no results. Then, a student is automatically provided an option to create a new request, via which the student may post a concise and clear question. Code may also be directly copied and pasted, and so may even error and bug messages /code.

All requests are processed using NLP to auto-tag to the course outline. These tags, in return also form the search auto-suggestions. With AI-like processing approach, the App is simple and effective to use.

6. Plans to further develop the initiative

Though the app was concept tested in an open app show event, in front of a wider university audience including the HOD of the DCSE, senior delegates from the University, faculty and students from various departments - there is more to be done. There are minor aspects related to set-up, and there also are significant human aspects, such as working with a wider audience to address their lack of exposure to anything like this before.

Next three steps:
1. To reduce set-up efforts, to allow addition of more courses and classes on the fly
2. To enhance functionality for more dynamic configurability (e.g. adding and removing faculty, guest faculty and the roles they can play etc.)
3. To seek university wide deployment

References

Diversity has been recognized as a valid academic concern. Several universities and organizations seeking equal opportunity have recognized the importance of managing diversity and have listed similar diversity challenges, their approaches to managing diversity in classrooms and learning outcomes openly in their online student centers and faculty teaching guides. We list key references that helped uncover a much wider case than we initially started with.

Bart, M. 2016 ."Diversity and Inclusion in the College Classroom". Magna Publications USA.
     Available at: http://provost.tufts.edu/celt/files/Diversity-and-Inclusion-Report.pdf
Bennett, C. and Rockwell K. 1995. "Targeting Outcomes for Programs: A Hierarchy for
     Targeting Outcomes and Evaluating Their Achievement", University of Nebraska.
     Available at ftp://bsesrv214.bse.vt.edu/grisso/Program_Logic/Targeting_Outcome_P
     rogramming.pdf.
Garibay J.C. 2015 . "Creating a positive classroom climate for diversity". Available at:
     https://equity.ucla.edu/wp-
     content/uploads/2016/06/CreatingaPositiveClassroomClimateWeb-2.pdf

Society for Diversity America 2017."Integration Isn't Easy", Society for Diversity America.
Available at: http://www.societyfordiversity.org/importance-of-diversity-in-the-classroom/
Yale 2019. "Diversity in the Classrooms", Yale Poorvu Center for Teaching and Learning.
Available at: https://poorvucenter.yale.edu/teaching/ideas-teaching/diversity-classroom, downloads: Diversity Problem Scenarios

Author Biography

Nitin Varma is an industry-academic data science Professor at Chitkara University, Punjab India. Nitin's ~25 years since graduation include global IT consulting for Fortune 500 organizations such as IBM, SAP and with cutting edge technologies for Smart Cities. Nitin is an Engineer (NITK), MBA (SPJIMR) and Doctorate(IIM Ranchi – Information Systems) and likes to explore innovative solutions across business domains

Piotr Wisniewski, Ph.D. and Chartered MCSI - is a dynamic, cosmopolitan business executive, combining financial industry expertise and international academia, currently also an Associate Professor at the Institute of Finance, Warsaw School of Economics Poland. Piotr is a manager, lecturer, entrepreneur, consultant, researcher, planner and author who keeps busy generating imaginative business and financial solutions across segments

www.ingramcontent.com/pod-product-compliance
Lightning Source LLC
LaVergne TN
LVHW012333060326
832902LV00011B/1872